Kaleidoscope

Dallas Hembra

Praise for *Kaleidoscope*

"To say Dallas Hembra has a way with words, is an understatement. *Kaleidoscope* is well-rounded and colorfully varied. It is thought provoking, raw, and passionate, awakening the senses to things we may have taken for granted. A joy to read."

—Renee Salvatori, Author of *Open Your Heart to the True You*

Kaleidoscope

A Rich and Varied Treasure of Poetic Gemstones

Dallas Hembra

Green Bay, WI

***Kaleidoscope*: A Rich and Varied Treasure of Poetic Gemstones** by Dallas Hembra, copyright © 2020 by Dallas Hembra. The poems "Alcohol" and "Crossing the Bridge" were previously published in *Shaking the Family Tree*, reprinted with the author's permission. Author photos courtesy of the Hembra family, © 2019 by the Hembra family. Cover art design, interior layout design, chapter head artwork, and the Written Dreams logo © 2019 by Written Dreams Publishing. This book reflects the opinions of the author and her life's decisions. Written Dreams Publishing does not approve, condone, or disapprove of these opinions.

All rights reserved. In accordance with the U.S. Copyright Act of 1976, no part of this publication may be reproduced, distributed, or transmitted in any form or by any means, or stored in a database or retrieval system, without prior written permission of the publisher, Written Dreams Publishing, Green Bay, Wisconsin 54311. Please be aware that if you've received this book with a "stripped" off cover, please know that the publisher and the author may not have received payment for this book, and that it has been reported as stolen property. Please visit www.writtendreams.com to see more of the unique books published by Written Dreams Publishing.

Publishing Editor: Brittiany Koren
Copy-editor: A.L. Mundt
Cover Art Designer: Sunny Fassbender
Print Interior Layout Designer: Katy Brunette
Ebook Interior Layout Designer: Maria Connor

Category: Poetry
Description: Single author collection of poetry about real life issues.
Paperback ISBN: 978-1-951375-18-8
Ebook ISBN: 978-1-951375-19-5
LOC Catalogue Data: Applied for.

First Edition published by Written Dreams Publishing in March, 2020.

Green Bay, WI 54311

Dear Reader,

Random meanderings intended to touch the heart, tickle the funny bone, awake the imagination, and in some cases, give pain a voice.

Kaleidoscope, unlike many other poetry chapbooks, is not theme driven. It is a multi-faceted look through the prism of life's resplendent observation tower. It explores the mountainous terrains of love and heartache, giggles at the ridiculous, stokes our anger, and acknowledges our fears. *Kaleidoscope* randomly selects pieces of our puzzles and arranges them in a panoramic lens that shapes our shared experiences.

It is arranged in four sections. Each includes a very brief description of the various forms of poetry found within.

And a little sidebar here for the traditionalists: there are a few instances where I may have taken liberties with or diverted from a particular form for the sake of expression.

Dallas Hembra

February, 2020

Section 1

Haiku:

A haiku is an unrhymed Japanese poetic form that usually consists of seventeen syllables arranged in three lines containing five, seven, and five syllables respectively. It almost always refers to nature and is intended to paint a picture in as few words as possible. The third line is often an "*aha*" moment. Fewer syllables are also acceptable, but must be a short, long, short movement. Haikus are written in the present tense. A haiku suite is a combination of three or more haikus.

Senryu:

A senryu has an identical structure to a haiku. It has three lines. The first line has five syllables. The second line has seven syllables. The third line has five syllables also. Senryus, unlike haikus, are primarily concerned with human nature, often humorous or satiric. A non-traditional senryu can have less than 5/7/5 syllables. A common variation is 3/5/3.

Tanka:

A tanka is another poetry type related to the haiku. The first three lines are unrhymed. They have a syllable count of five, seven, five like the haiku. But the last two lines both have seven syllables. So, the syllable count is: (5/7/5/7/7.) The third line is a pivotal line that could end lines one and two and/or begin lines four and five.

All of these forms usually refrain from having punctuation and capitalization, except for proper nouns.

Cheating Daylight

gray ominous sky
decides to pull the shades down
winter solstice

Birthing Autumn

sun glows—subtle slant
summer releasing its grasp
announcing autumn

Monsoon Rains

monsoon rains
infuse plants—cause root rot
drowning victims

Gossip

she mutes lip's remote
when enticed to spread gossip
woman of substance

Brazen Blue Jay

brazen blue jay
chases cardinal from feeder
backyard bully

Snow Clings to Bark

snow clings to bark
gently drapes dark slender limbs
man in moon approves

Good-bye Kiss

winter's rogue snowflake
plants a gentle parting kiss
on perplexed pansy

Super Moon

super moon suits up
polices dark lover's leap
nocturnal flashlight

Autumn Eulogy

beat-up rusty rake
assembles withering leaves
autumn eulogy

Dallas Hembra

Autumn

school bus waits

for mom to zip up hoodie

frost on her pumpkin

dreams steeped in cider

rekindle old memories

fire in the furnace

blackbirds hover

as scarecrow naps on the job

carpe diem

Compositions

April shower

dances on the roof

pinging in the rain

the roll of thunder

engages summer sizzle

sacred drumming

buzzing inside hive

produces masterpiece

taste of honey

Trickle-Down

a strong work ethic
becomes a family trait
trickle-down theory

Cleaving

October morning
primed in patchwork promises
shuns a hint of frost

Spirit of Winter

bold winter spirit
prowls the mountains of Tibet
stalking snow leopard

Hope Snuffed

a newborn's future
sabotaged inside the womb
addict's legacy

Kids' Win

snow shovel idle
kids playing video games
mom gives in again

Self-diminished

self diminishes
as soul selects expansion
in God's universe

The Voting Booth

new sign at the polls
searching for integrity?
check junk folder

Copycats

a new set of rules
for political debates
no more lip-syncing

Mislaid Memory

mislaid memory
fights its way to the surface
old man reels it in

Shhhh

spiritual growth
doing the next right thing
anonymously

Windsong

above his headstone
swinging from a shepherd's hook
wind chimes chase silence

Across the Miles

another grandchild
born across too many miles
chain of missing links

Sunburn

sunburned child
in unprotected sandbox
mommy naps in shade

Winter's Weight

beneath winter's weight
broken branches lay scattered
grave of fractured limbs

Dark Cumulus Clouds

dark cumulus clouds
assault a clear azure sky
bruised palette

Dallas Hembra

Last Slice of Pie

savoring the crumbs—
inside time's constraints
my last slice of pie

Halloween All Year Round

costumed candidates
in race to recalibrate
trot out tricks and tweets

One Night Stand

the pulse of passion
fading in the light of day
empty wine bottles
drained dry in desperation
reeking of reality

Comatose

ten seasons muted
cast adrift in stalled shadows
a silenced remote
still records signs of aging
comatose patient turns gray

Zebra

shades of Africa
create a cloud of thunder
a herd of zebras
splash across the savannah
black on white blurs white on black

Abandoned Trellis

abandoned trellis
left in overgrown garden
a fading eyesore
leans against old stone wall
befriends fragile climbing rose

Transparency

wrapped in cellophane
stored away in dark closets
the transparency
of every politician's
potential embarrassment

Wake-up Call

brought to our knees by
atmospheric conditions
rearranging life
Mother Nature coaxes us
to take on global warming

His Pledge

another new dawn
dances on her horizon
in a blaze of youth
he pledges her his vision
of rocking chairs and sunsets

Don't Rush Her

pounding on her door
clothed in a December frown
winter rants and raves
blind to the fact that autumn
has yet to shed her attire

Cold Shoulder

arctic air attack
generates fresh open wound
lover's berating
turns into crystallized pain
emotional ice sculpture

Veteran's Day

every veteran
writes freedom across the land
flags—red, white, and blue
unfurled in recognition
band heroes past and present

Footprints

I feel your footprints
tiptoeing across my soul
light as a feather
they are floating on the breeze
comforting my broken heart

Fall's Dying Embers

fall's dying embers
pressed into my diary
memories waiting
for the pages to be turned
their spirits resurrected

Section II

Haibun:

The haibun is another Japanese form. It is a prose poem interweaved with one or more haiku. It is composed of three elements: title, prose, and haiku. The haiku, which can be injected anywhere in the body of the prose, should be relative but abstract. The prose is not an explanation of the haiku. The haiku is not a linear continuation of the prose.

Haibun usually take you on a journey, either physical or mental. They may record a scene or a special moment in a highly descriptive and objective manner, or may occupy a wholly fictional or dreamlike space.

There are many rules that govern the haibun, and once again, if the author has skirted any of them for the sake of expression, she apologizes to traditionalists.

A Graveside Visit

curiosity
festers in my growing need
to find myself

Dear Grandma Allen,

How dare I tread on the brittle frozen earth that covers your history after all of these years? Why now, the sudden interest to get to know you? You have been gone fifty some years. I wasn't even sure I could find your headstone. Daisy, Lottie Allen: born May 1886—entered into rest January 1964.

Daisy. What a bright, evocative image that conjures. Wish that is how I remembered you, instead of an invisible and undefined Lottie; a picture Mom had a hand in painting. I have so many questions spinning around in my head; stupid ones, like did you have the right to vote in 1920 when Mom was born? Who picked out your old lady dresses and cut your hair in such a nondescript style? Was it Aunt Mimi or you? And why didn't you make everyone at the dinner table wait to eat until you sat down, after serving them? The memory of you eating alone, seated at the same table everyone else had turned their back on and vacated, is embedded in my mind, an embarrassment to this day.

I used to get angry when Mom and Aunt Mimi would refer to you as dull or not too bright. Later, I wondered, were those perceptions correct? And could they have been a precursor to your Alzheimer's? I wouldn't have labeled you so unkindly. Passive perhaps, and definitely oppressed. Something or someone stifled your voice from ever developing. You wilted and died a Lottie, without ever blooming into a daisy.

        links to the past
    buried in the unturned soil
          of apathy

Equilibrium

        photoshoot
     before fog lifts
       out of focus

Maybe if I squint and stand back far enough, I'll get a better perspective when I look through the black hole that follows the twists and turns bleeding on my canvas. I need to see which areas are out of balance.

    It's all about balance. *That's what they say, isn't it,* the great gurus sitting behind their psychology?

    But life isn't like a painting, where you can fill in the empty space with more empty space. Or just tint it another shade, and then pollute the corresponding sides with needless trinkets to offset it.

          gymnast
   topples from horse
         instability

Let's see. Too much booze and not enough V-8. Maybe I can fix that, maybe!

    Countless affairs but no real relationships; that's a biggie, better put that in the questionable column. Too much work and not enough play; wonder if they give lessons for that? Numerous religious forays seeking spirituality, not found. Doesn't look real promising.

    Maybe tomorrow I'll start with a blank canvas, or better yet, jump on an addiction that will tip the scale in my favor.

           warning
 clean slate buried beneath
         black ice

My Love/Hate Relationship

That warm, familiar slant of fall is settling in. I feel it roosting deep inside my solar plexus as it tweaks and tugs at my dormant melancholy. God's perfect dichotomy lurking just around the corner. The clash of magnificent beauty pitted against a menacing cloud of migratory depression…

Why? What's the purpose? How is it that while bathing in its ardent splendor, I sink into the depths of vulnerability? No pause in between: simultaneously.

It's a symbiotic relationship that makes no sense to me. One minute I'm tap-dancing for joy in autumn's frothing radiance. The next, I'm bending into the pallor of obscurity. Like curling leaves, my nerves turn inside out. All that I am, or am not, will be mutually exposed for all the world to see. Maybe I am bipolar. Must remember to ask the doctor. There are meds for that.

>autumn's offering
>playing on the doorstep
>of my sanity

But, not to worry. It's only August; summer will linger for a while. Still have plenty of time to fine-tune my nature in preparation for my *favorite* season.

>smooth sailing
>without a few waves
>leads to dead sea

Alcohol

*Previously published in *Shaking the Family Tree*

I've trudged many miles to get to this: my vanishing point. I have not traveled alone. I drag behind me generations of my kind. We often travel in packs, keeping others at bay, hoarding our secret. The vast terrain that has claimed many of us is strewn with the souls of those who sought escape from poverty, abuse, low self-esteem, and life in general. We found a magic elixir. It became our family's coat of arms.

>seduction
>hides inside a goddess
>Venus flytrap

For a while, it erased our fears and insecurities. We gulped greedily from its promise as it seeped through the cracks in our armor. We dressed in layers of false courage, fluffed our feathers and strutted across life's stage, immune to the snickers of a disgusted audience. We cast aside our problems, and they became the property of those we loved. Then, without warning, it betrayed us.

>heir declines offer
>cannot afford to pay
>inheritance tax

Dallas Hembra

Crossing the Bridge

*Previously published in *Shaking the Family Tree*

One by one, they circled the parameter of sobriety. Driven from their comfort zone by the scent of death and the gravity of isolation, the pack became fragmented. It was no longer cohesive. It couldn't protect them from the inevitable. As they clambered across the bridge of uncertainty, the escapees paused and cast pleading glances across the abyss, encouraging the other members to join them.

But it wasn't their time. The wounds weren't deep enough, the scars not yet committed to the annals of shame and regret.

> the force of the storm
> doesn't always rip away
> every leaf that clings

Those who dare to take a leap into that scary, unknown territory called sobriety have a long, hard fight ahead. Every one step forward is often followed by two steps backward. People, places, and things have to be changed and new support systems erected in their places. Mental and physical cravings must be dealt with. Facing life on life's terms without a substance to rely on requires a commitment to self that goes beyond the norm. The process of getting sober can be a tug of war. But the rewards are so numerous and the joy so overwhelming, that a few rope burns are a small price to pay.

> a taste of spring
> followed by a harsh winter
> season of hope

Gaps

Must be a rupture somewhere. It feels like my glass is always half empty. A tear in the fabric of my memory where pieces of the day's puzzle keep falling out. *Kerplunk.* There goes another one! It's the one that belongs to that thing up on the wall.

What's it called? Uh…um. That's it. Got it. The date keeper. Wonder if it fell in the same hole as the name of the street I live on? Yesterday, or was it today, somebody who called himself my son asked if I took my medicine. How the hell do I know?

No more water in the glass. "Maybe!"

>   deep inside the fog
>   a quiet serenity
>   calms the confusion

Bookmarks

Draw the shades and close your eyes. Sink into the comfort of little effort, and I will open up my book to you. Hand in hand, we will traverse the chapters of an untold life. Relax in my sporadic ramblings and be grateful that grief has yet to appear on your pages.

In the beginning, the print that spells me is fresh off the press. It spills onto my palette in a range of vibrant colors that beg to bloom on my yet untarnished composition.

As I grow, I glide across synchronized sentences, unblemished and unafraid. But soon the ink begins to run. It trickles down tattered paper in a river of black bewilderment, wearing away my fairytale.

Time and circumstance begin to punish me. They stain me till I become a jaundiced history of curled pages abandoned to obscurity.

> in the library
> a shaft of sunlight magnifies
> the emptiness

Summer Musings

Vowels, soft as rose petals drifting on the breeze, fauna, flora. Delicate whisperings tease my imagination, as auditory visions flutter in duplicity, filling my senses. A locust shell shed on the tree bark in a cacophony of noise... August singing.

Adjectives, sweltering heat, fresh mown grass, cobalt-blue skies mingle with the white linen sheets blowing on the clothesline. Gangly brown clothes props, notched to perfection by Dad, lined up like sentinels, doing their job. Memories of Mom, spilling from a tumbler, tucked away in yesterday. Yesterday, a safe harbor in a bustling port.

Ouch, the beginning of a headache. A mallet splintering my reverie. Shattered diamonds spilling on time's parched soil.

> summer daydreams
> squelched in the reality
> of a pending storm

Dallas Hembra

The Beauty of Ordinary

As today comes to an end, I realize that I no longer need chaos to put me to bed. The need to escape life no longer chases me around the confines of yesterday's cellblock. Fear and anxiety, where are you? Are you still lurking in the seams of my new garments? The ones that I am growing comfortable in?

    Delusion. I see through your camouflage. Highs disguised as fun, lust whispering love. And excitement that nearly drove me over the edge. Tonight, as I sink my soul into a softer pillow, I will coax my dreams to unfold in a gentler hue.

contentment
thrives in blushing garden
peace presides

The camera's rolling. Capturing the subtle nuances of my morning. Hazelnut coffee in my favorite mug, a squirrel scampering up the mighty oak outside my window. I can almost touch the gratitude I feel for this changed perspective as I saunter to the porch. My new awareness breathes in the fragrance of the roses as they scale the sun-dappled trellis, and I sense serenity stroking me awake. With a cleansed heart, I accept the invitation to unwrap an extraordinary day.

Rooted in Time

platonic shifts
on my Richter scale—
holding on

Periodically, I stumble upon a relic from the past. One that is situated in some far-off corner of my mind. A physical benchmark that has neither evolved nor eroded. One that remains steadfast, holding its ground, in spite of the many changes surrounding it. Left exactly where it placed its foothold many moons ago. And I celebrate, sipping the sweet taste of nostalgia.

    These brushes with yesterday's dust replenish me. They have no emotional significance in and of themselves. They can be as mundane as an old moss-covered stone wall that survived the destruction of the home it shored up. Or a light tower poised on the highest peak of a hill that continues to stand guard over the forlorn, empty lot where my grade school once stood.

wrapped in a blanket
of familiarity
serenity sighs

Dallas Hembra

The Art of Back and Forth

Just another ordinary day, sitting all alone on the porch swing. Feels like a storm's brewing. The air is hot and sultry, like the touch of Jeb's warm, sweet breath caressing the nape of my neck. Now, whatever made me think of that? He's been gone over ten years now. Snapped up like a kidnapped victim, in the prime of his life. God, it's going to be a long day.

flies buzzing round
busy little bastards
swat—

Wind's picking up. Would you look at that wheat over there in the field, swaying to and fro like it was in some kind of hypnotic trance, a summer waltz with no lyrics? Big as you were, Jeb, you were the smoothest dancer on the floor, all 310 pounds of you.

drifting in and out—
euphoric anesthetic
brings relief

Springs in this old swing must need oiling; it sounds like his muffled snoring. Such a foolish idea, thinking if he burrowed 'neath the covers it wouldn't keep me awake.
  The honeysuckle is just starting to bloom, but it can't hold a candle to that fancy bottle of Aramis still sitting on his dresser.

long winding roads
open invitation
to disappear

My Epitaph

I wonder where these insane musings originate. In my brain or in my boredom?

Here I sit at my expansive desk with its five-foot extension, using the half-hour allotted me for lunch to ponder my eight-by-eight foot workspace to wonder if I were to suddenly kick the bucket, what would it say about me? Would the myriad of scattered photos that dominate the desk, are taped to the walls, and that have spilled over into the drawers testify to the fact I have been a good grandmother? Boy, was that a God gift. My second chance to get it right and I didn't blow it.

That Anne Geddes replica of two little cherubs, sisters in their innocence—surely that won't go unnoticed. Everyone knows how close Mimi and I are. Complete opposites by nature, but twins in spirit.

Oh, and the organization—the stack of neat folders, the pens and pencils standing at attention in the oversized mug, the post-it notes all color-coordinated that decorate the space between my keyboard and monitor. That ought to get me some brownie points, at least until someone opens my drawers and discovers that they are jammed with reams of five-year-old correspondence. Hey, you never know when something might come back to bite you in the ass. Gotta be prepared, that's my motto.

Whoops, time's up. Back to work.

sun goes down
in a blaze of color
shadows hover

Dallas Hembra

Bump in the Road

The well's run dry. Don't think I can squeeze another syllable out of this stagnant reservoir. Even the mundane musings have turned to silt. Help, someone throw me some *floaties*. I'm drowning in my own inertia. My pen needs a rest; it's grown weary of the endless tug of war that takes place inside my confused concept of creativity. A tired lament imitating yesterday's voice hovers, stuck on the turntable of humdrum, the needle's dull ache echoing my dying determination.

hungry artist
dips into jellybean jar
comes up empty-handed

Twinkle, twinkle, rising star; I do wonder where you are. Suffocating in this void, growing even more annoyed. Now, there's a catchy phrase.
   Where the hell did I pitch that pen? Screw it.
   Broken thoughts keep tripping over missing Scrabble tiles. I don't want to play anymore. I concede.

white flag unfurls
beneath angry red sky
bloodstained surrender

Saturday Afternoons

Fun times being broadcasted onto a childhood's memory stick. Ten silver spokes. Flip-flop-toss. Soft, pink rubber balls bounce better than glossy-painted red ones. Sisters' butts glued to the kitchen's cheap linoleum floor. Cool and soothing on bare sun-tanned legs, dressed in short shorts. Sun smiling its approval through white eyelet curtains. Mom at work. Out of sight and earshot. Can't hear jacks spreading their joy during postponed chores.

stolen moments
wrestled from obligations
siblings' covert reward

Deft hands sweep up win. Sissy cries foul! "You touched one. I saw it move." Argument ensues. Clock ticks peace and quiet away. Storm brews outside as competition rages inside. Mom due home soon. We gather up our jacks and agree to just one game of pick-up sticks.

pockets of pleasure
placed in yesterday's storage
long-term memory

Unhinged

Up, down, back and forth. Flailing in space devoid of tangibles. Nothing to cling to as I go bouncing around in the invisible chaos.

Black sky. White sky. No sky! Blood clouds rolling overhead. Cursing me in sinister, silent gestures. Felt a splat. Stings like a slap. Crimson droplets hemorrhaging, leaving me awash in life's swollen indifference.

Seeking a foothold in this ether world. But there is no ground to be found. Can't touch down.

Tethered to nothing, I dangle in the tangles of disconnected pathways, praying for a set of wings to offset the muddied impression of another patient's disjointed foot dragging around these hallucinations.

bending moments
racing the inevitable
round the final stretch

Static

The lightning is grounding. Here comes the *kaboom*. My head is pounding. Social media onomatopoeia, an encroaching cancer on steroids.

  The peal of hate pinging, ringing the bell in the belfry of my sensibilities. Unfriend me, please. I'm begging you. Yank me, and I'll yank you. Tit for tat, turn off the chat. All that garbage exploding on your page is seeping into my bludgeoned respect for you.

  I feel contaminated. Where the hell is the brain sanitizer? A sonic stink is drumming disharmony into yesterday's friendship. What happened to your hushed tranquility? I can't find it. Is it hiding under the soiled sheets that changed your bed? Hey! Can you hear me beneath the din of fake news and the vibration of four-lettered vulgarities? Hey…hey.

dreaded decision
spikes as brain waves are muted
time to pull the plug

Selections

My life is an enigma. It unfolds to the rhythm of my moods. Every day, I reach into my wardrobe and choose from a variety of fabrics vying for my attention. Snickering, they lay in wait, dangling from the unhinged mind that coddles them. Some are drab. They droop at the notion of putting forth any effort. Others, remnants of the past, beckon me to slip into some kind of a bipolar dance of unpleasant memories. They are crimson convulsions of anger, yellow-striped hues of fear, and heavy titanium armor meant to keep the world at bay, to battle to forge my identity.

misery
writes its epitaph
in shades of choice

But hiding in the wrinkled folds of change, pastel shades of new beginnings shake up the status quo. A ripple of reason emerges. Serenity drapes its quiet message over the bellowing negatives, tucking them in for a much-needed rest. And in the midst of this flurry of finery, I find myself grabbing hold of a positive day.

Author's Note:

This brings to an end the section devoted to my favorite form, the haibun. As for myself, unlike many other forms, I have found that the haibun cannot be written on demand. Instead, I must wait patiently for it to let me know when it wants to be penned.

Section III

Free Verse:

Free verse is a form of poetry that does not necessarily follow any specific meter, rhyme, or other pattern.

Free verse, despite its freedom, often has some elements of form. Most free verse does observe a convention of lines and structure. Alliteration, metaphor, personification, and simile are often employed.

The Unforgiven

Shattered values lay seeping
in a reservoir of soul's emptiness,
stagnation slowing life's steadfast flow.

Shame stabs at her fragility—
etching puncture wounds
mapped in tattooed shades of goth,
while rectitude bides time on bended knee
beneath the altar of repentance.

Cast adrift on the silent sea of retribution
pondering past transgressions,
she howls at the waning moon—
engraved in its total eclipse.

The Calm Before the Storm

The rising sun stretched across the water's surface
yawning the arrival of yesterday's promise;
climbing, it scatters its shimmering glitter
on dimpled waves lapping against the shore.

On the horizon, a majestic ocean liner
gracefully skates across the blue meridian;
trawlers, drifting holograms, dot the distance
framed by a school of frolicking porpoises.

The beach is teeming with nature's early risers
sandpipers and seagulls
basking in the solitude,
enjoying the quiet that will quiver
in the stampeding of flip-flops,
the thrust of cumbersome umbrellas,
and the cutting edge of aluminum
being dragged across the virgin sand
scarring the serenity.

Dallas Hembra

Road Trip

Bleached sheets
billow in the breeze
of
simplicity;
lace curtains invite daybreak;
framed in palpable pride
picture-perfect lawns
manicured
by
mild-mannered women
steeped in tradition.
Passing horse and buggy—
entering
Amish country.

Autonomy

The calligraphy
that propels passion
dissolving yesterday's dogma,
submerged in the baptismal font
of new beliefs;
old ideas
coded in genetic chips
short circuit—
creating seasons of unwritten pages.

An empty portfolio
waits
to be pollinated
by the secretion of self,
freed of family flavor,
unscripted by society,
devoid of all others' debris.

Autonomy—the calligraphy that pens my character.

Dallas Hembra

Dementia

Adrift—
like dying leaves
no longer able
to cleave to branches
twisted and tangled—
memories desert a mind
no longer able
to sustain or retain
a face
an embrace
a time when wined and dined;
brilliance fading beneath the weight
of a loved one's aching.
No longer able
to keep pace
with changing patterns
as all around,
leaves crunch
in autumn's wake.

Death of Diplomacy

Atmospheric changes—
tepid conditions heating up
moving
in concentric circles
gathering grimaces,
cutting through furrowed brows
and
cryptic contradictions.
Nuclear agreement—
dissolving in volcanic ash
spews its residue
across a planet
already buried
in biohazardous bullshit.

Dallas Hembra

Life Is Fragile

Life is fragile
a
wondering wisp
tethered to time.
Cushion its delicacy
inhale
the jasmine moments
funneled through
rose-petaled pleasures
hiding
behind shears of uncertainty.
Breathe in, breathe out
relax in its rhythm
absorb its aroma,
ponder the question of porcelain propositions.
This life is fragile—
a feather blowing in the breeze;
dally in its descending.

Boundaries

Stretched across an alien landscape
hers remain invisible,
blending and bleeding
indiscernible—
lacking definition.
Challengers gain entry—
seeping through the cracks
of a brave fading reserve
like sludge—
sliding down the slippery slope
of naivety.
Lofty attempts
to stand vertical
on a horizontal doormat,
destined to failure
in the all-too-familiar world
of camouflaged angles.

Everlasting

Love
allows us to linger
in pastel hues,
enhancing the taste of tenderness
in the buds
of memories sweet—
soothing our starving palate;
love
tucks itself inside
whispered hauntings
where
perfumed melodies
float
on plein air clouds—
hovering
above our fading shadows,
promising to repair
tomorrow's broken heart.

Parallel Paths

The year is aging
in hues of red and gold—
wrinkled leaves
being crushed
underfoot
by this weary time traveler.

As they float and flutter
toward their decomposition,
the thought of brittle bones
turning to dust
winds and wends its way
through my morbidity.

Shuddering,
I shuffle through the mounting heap,
drifting in and out of December's
merging specter—
trying to tune out
my calendar's cacophony.

Wind's wrath waits round the corner
biding its time,
receding into the temporary reprieve;
I proceed to procrastinate.

Rainbow Reflection

I am reflected in a rainbow
where I wonder weightlessly,
tethered neither to time
nor
boundaries.
My presence is a pantomime
living in a lover's laughter,
a fragrance
remembered in a rose.
I inhale
incredulous concerns
and exhale eternity,
relinquishing ego
trapped in the shattered
traces
of life's looking glass.
I am reflected in a rainbow,
presumed in a prayer.

The Finish Line

Time slipping from her grasp—
fleet of foot;
it runs across
the fields of her youth,
ducking under broken bridges,
seeping through forgotten
cracks of opportunities,
plowing pastures
of love unearthed.
A backward glance
cradles her apparition
in a translucent tear;
"Come on,
I can't slow down—
it's against the rules.
Hurry,
catch me if you can."
The echo fades
into retreating shadows;
she slips gently from its grasp
watching time run out.

Dallas Hembra

Suspended

Suspended
in the in-between time
where
a flurry of activity
no longer flutters.
How I long to slip
between life's folds
where
but a flaccid response
is all that's required
in a languid land
where
all for naught
is the only duty sired,
where
even a whisper remains retired.
In the in-between time
where rest is restored
on the cusp of what's next
and postponement becomes
tomorrow's reward.

Obscurity

Heads never turn
eyes don't light up
no one ever notices—
one must look hard to see ordinary;
no bells
no whistles;
desperation resides undetected.
A special delivery label
doesn't adorn our persona.
We don't
stand out in a crowd
or
manifest in small gatherings.
Falling off the edge
has become an art.
As we topple down
life's elevator shaft,
our muffled screams
leave behind trailing echoes
as we are swallowed up
by
anonymity.

Dallas Hembra

The Footprint

Faith fought hard to embed its footprint
on the ocean floor of his doubt.
It wrestled the waves and riptides—
sustained its strength with each new bout
while it mocked the moon at high tide.
Faith understood the grace of depth,
so it burrowed even deeper
as the storm brewed on the surface
where shallow creeds
cast a shadow on the fray.
Somewhere in the depths of uncertainty,
a shift in impetus began to take hold—
the rise and fall of the soul
inhaling the calm,
exhaling the struggle,
spawning a seismic transformation,
permitting faith to instill its footprint.

Love's Sixth Sense

The cutting edge of distrust
sharpens its scissors,
slicing and shredding its way across
the fabric of her suspicions.

Neon flashes—
sealed behind closed eyes
flutter in variegated hues of lilting love,
while twisted words tumble,
slowly slipping through the perforated lining
of her naivety.

Rotting in the shadows,
the stench of deceit festers,
tweaking its talons on lascivious lies
revised in rehearsal.

Sirens scream, begging her to awaken—
to forsake distorted fantasies,
tempting her to taste
the bittersweet reality
breaking on morn's shore.

Her gut's final entreaty
to entrust his deception
to the enticement
of the outgoing tide.

Lost Lyrics

The storage bin bides empty
but the stench of loss
permeates what's been abandoned.
Deep in the forest
of forgotten phrases
words wind aimlessly about
in a game of hide and seek
calling
catch me if you can.
Echoes of forgotten fervor
bounce
off the walls of frustration
where imprisoned in a vacuum of dead silence—
vibrations
haunt the halls of lost lyrics.

A Garden of Mourners

The day she was buried
dew
dampened her roses;
it streamed down the sturdiest of stems
supporting the wilting petals
gathered at her grave;
drenched in mourning,
a plethora of colorful annuals
that popped up once a year
shared space
with
a smattering of stalwart perennials
embedded in the ecosystem,
defying excavation,
entitled to endowments.

Dirty Laundry

Through tepid, porous promises
trust trickles,
dressed in silver-plated words
not worth a nickel.
Your reputation's been
hung out to dry.
See it swaying on that slumping
line of lies?
Hear it
drip
drip
  D
    R
      I
        P
          P
        I
      N
    G
Dirty laundry.

Invisible

Your anguish drives me to my pen. We've never met, but my lens has captured you in passing on the street, in the supermarket,
standing in line at the bank.

Your image is stored in the darkroom of my soul. I've shied away from your blank gaze, your turned-down head; I've bowed my own head, straining to hear your apologetic whispers as you try to explain to human services your very existence.

There are days I've even tasted your poverty at the checkout counter as you empty your cart of cheap hot dogs and mac and cheese to feed your family of five.

Perhaps I've not walked in your shoes. But I have lived enough pieces of your life to recognize that beneath the battering, the bruising, and the clutching to your anonymity, there lurks a hero. A butterfly waiting to unfold, searching for it wings. And someone to simply *acknowledge* your plight so that you might take flight.

Dallas Hembra

Remembering Joy

Joy
tasted snowflakes
tap-dancing on the tip of a child's tongue.

Joy
listened for the echo of sleigh bells
gaining ground in imagination's anticipation.

Joy
inhaled the scent of love,
wafting from a warm plate of Christmas cookies baked
in a busy oven.

Joy
hitched rides on Radio Flyers
speeding down snow-packed slopes;
lit the candles,
infused the glow,
whispered the prayers that engraved hope's signature on
yesterday's Christmas card.

Muddy Waters

Muddy waters wait
for me
stalk me
tucked inside REM
deep beneath my pillow;
yesterday's creek rises
flooding my landscape
through
time's placenta.
Mom's frenetic accusation froths
wave after wave
germinates guilt
your fault
she almost died
your fault
Muddy waters rising
blonde ringlets
flotsam
floating on hell's surface
wearing my sister's name—
the burden of being the oldest
clawing at my six years.

Dallas Hembra

Beginnings

Love
believes in beginnings—
the phenomenon of a poem's first draft,
a blank canvas begging to be set ablaze.
Love
belongs to the rhythm of inception
where
compositions wait to be written
and
rituals don't have to rhyme—
where
reason is but a magician's illusion
on tomorrow's stage.
Love
avoids veiled endings,
tangled in bolts of black and white design
that
end up on the cutting room floor,
severed from forgotten beginnings.

Ecstasy

A
smattering of stardust
falls
across the weathered pages
of
malleable meanderings
called yesterday.
Tensions turn inside out
as
you ruffle rambling
memories,
pinning passion to poetry—
weaving whispers
into
the fabric of pleasure's
portal.
As
dusk settles the dust
behind curtained windows,
secrets
crawl beneath the covers
to be
tucked away for eternity.

Dallas Hembra

Street Child

Street child
how
to fill the vacancy
reflected
in
your hollow gaze?
a
barren stretch of sadness
where unoccupied
has become an instant messenger,
unable to locate a server
to deliver your plea
to a world
so preoccupied
that it turns its head
in passing
as you
pander your pain,
postured
in
subtle supplication.

Puzzled

Bits and pieces of me
scattered in disarray,
lost in the flurry
of your emotional limitations,
slated for the scrap heap
with no one
to catch my spilling tears
from your indifference
as they stain my soul.
No one
to embrace my pain
as it breaks up the framework
of my fantasy,
and
no one
to gather up
the frayed warped pieces
and arrange me whole again,
piecing together my puzzled concepts
that no longer fit snugly
into the cornerstone
of us.

Section IV

Rhyme, and a variety of other forms:

Cinquain:

A cinquain has five lines, as "cinq" is French for the number five. Each line follows a specific pattern. The traditional cinquain has a strict structure based on syllable count.

> Line one: Two syllables
>
> Line two: Four syllables
>
> Line three: Six syllables
>
> Line four: Eight syllables
>
> Line five: Two syllables

Acrostic:

An acrostic is a poem that spells out a word or idea from top to bottom. It usually spells out the title of the poem itself. Each beginning letter is either capitalized or in bold type, which allows it to stand out from the rest of the sentence; therefore, the reader can see the title within the poem. Sometimes a space between the first letter and the following sentence is used for emphasis.

ABC poem:

An ABC poem is a five-line poem, normally written to express feelings. The first four lines begin with sequential letters, i.e. d e f g, m n o p, et cetera. The fifth line can be any letter of choice. Longer versions adhere to the same rules.

Nonet:

A nonet is a nine-line poem. The first line contains nine syllables, the next line has eight syllables, the next seven, and so forth. This continues until the last line (the ninth) has one syllable. Rhyme is optional. The sequence can also be inverted.

Naani:

The naani is one of India's most popular Telugu poems. Naani means an expression of one and all. It consists of four lines. The total lines consist of twenty to twenty-five syllables. The poem is not bound to a particular subject. Although, generally, it will incorporate subjects such as human relations and current statements.

Rictameter:

A rictameter is a nine-line poem. Each line has a specific number of syllables. The first line has two syllables. The next line has four. The next line has six. The next line has eight. The next line has ten. Then it works its way down again (eight, six, four, two). The last line is the same as the first.

Lune:

The lune, also known as the American haiku, was first created by poet Robert Kelly. It was the result of Kelly's frustration with the English haiku. It is a thirteen-syllable, self-contained poem that has five syllables in the first line, three syllables in the second line, and five syllables in the final line. Unlike haiku, there are no other rules.

Etheree:

The etheree is similar to the cinquain and the rictameter. It is a ten-line form ascending in syllable count for ten unrhymed lines. An etheree should focus on one idea or subject, giving a syllable count of one, two, three, four, five, six, seven, eight, nine, and ten.

Septolet:

The septolet has fourteen words. It is broken between two stanzas that make up the fourteen words. Each stanza can have seven words each, but that is not a requirement. Both stanzas are about the same thought and create a picture.

These are brief descriptions of the various forms. To learn more, you can refer to the individual forms.

Wrapped In Before

An ode to my mother, Pinky Shipley

Who is this stranger?
Wrapped in before
Her life became
Adulthood's chore
Smile unencumbered
Soul feather-light
Anticipates
Love's promised flight.
Her childlike trust
Makes my heart soar
When on Dad's arm
Wrapped in before.
Vague echoes of what used to be
Reverberate inside of me
A mystery preserved in time
Mom's magic moment—in her prime.

Dallas Hembra

Grieving

Dedicated to my father, Jesse J. Shipley, who left us April 27th, 2000.

Here we are again, Dad
Your daughters at your side
Towing the weight of your parting—
The sting of your passing, smarting.
Two sisters
Fondling
The tear-drenched fern
That somberly adorns
Your grass-stained blanket.
And though our grief escorts us
Our eyes this day are dry,
And we wonder what that says
If anything
About our capacity to cry.
The sun that once we basked in
Your smile so warm and kind,
Has set without our sanction
Leaving shards of gray behind.
If no tears today pose healing
Is our grief now safely tucked away?
Or will it spill again tomorrow
On a piercing sunlit day?

Paper Dolls

Paper doll musings—a blast from the past
dressed them in wonder—
why didn't it last?
Glamour-sharp scissors obeyed my deft hands
as I cut, crimped, and fastened to meet their demands;
a gold-gilded gown trimmed in sequined esteem
found a split in my lacking, burrowed into its seam.
Kick-ass stilettos and ruby red lips
form-fitting sweaters, curvaceous round hips
bashful boobs perky, bees in their hives
sashaying down runways, I breathed them alive.
The fantasy flourished but a moment or two
till childhood relinquished its *come hither* hue.

Dallas Hembra

Upside Down

The stars began to tumble down
they fell to Earth without a sound;
they warned the sky
the night before
to tuck those clouds
into a drawer;
the moon agreed,
the grand old dame,
that starlight
should not take the blame
for robbing Earth of its delight
and snuffing out Heaven's light.
For when they fell to Earth, you see
they dove into the deep blue sea;
now everything is turned around
one must be standing upside down.
To wish upon a star today
a boat must ferry you far away,
then gaze you down instead of up
drinking the light from the oceans' cup.

Gone

Days unfold in sheets of grey
December's shroud replaces May,
Ravens coat the sky above
Impaling hope on wings of a dove.
Your leaving cleaves unto lost dreams
My future splitting at the seams,
What heart is remedied by loss?
My burden bends beneath your cross.
A void appears where once we played
Dark shadows cling to love decayed,
The night descends without delay
Into the mist, you slip away.

Dallas Hembra

Romance Me

Take the challenge if you dare
Prove to me you really care.
Waste not your effort, nor my time
If you believe you're past your prime.
Romance is not defined by age
A broken needle on youth's gauge;
It can't be borrowed, bought, or sold
Its value measured not in gold.
Encased in layers of desire
It smolders till it catches fire;
Unleashed in silent swells it roars
Rapping on windows and on closed doors.
So, if you dare this challenge take
Romance me till I snap awake,
Then lay me down in year's decline
Explore the blush of finely-aged wine.

The Victim

Her faith in mankind frayed,
her trust in youth betrayed.

Accosted on a busy street
in the middle of the day,
she lay crumpled on the concrete
in her neighborhood's decay.

The blow delivered from behind
by a street punk clothed in hate
is embedded now forever
in a fear that won't abate.

Dead bolts in place, the curtains drawn
long held beliefs, forever gone.

Dallas Hembra

Unraveling

Fractured feelings strewn across
the cluttered stretch of
miles of miscommunication;
at the intersection
frayed filaments
of yesterday's dreams
unravel at the seams
exposing naked truths;
her trousseau has no texture
his armor has a hole—
the ornaments of marriage
lay buried
in the failure of their porous soil.

The Night the Sky Cried

It began as a gentle weeping
on a stagnant summer morn
the world, part of it sleeping
stoic, stagnant, parched, forlorn.

Throughout the day, the teardrops spilled
intensifying—gushing;
the creek beds and the rivers filled
to the weight of water rushing.

At dusk, the sky out of control
reigned over all the land;
undauntingly, it took its toll
a taunting tangent reprimand.

The voice of thunder blasted
throughout the pitch black night;
ensuing shards of lightning
did ignite a sky, now bright.

The night the sky cried o'er the land
Mother Nature was distraught
by all the disrespect of man
for her, and for all he'd wrought.

Dallas Hembra

Invisible Scars

Who extinguished her inner light,
exposed her to contagions blight?
Plucked away her self-esteem,
robbed her of youth's nuptial dreams?
If a trial were held today
would the guilty be convicted,
or would the lack of evidence
set him free as he predicted?
A broken nose, a busted lip—
or perhaps some faded bruises,
might generate a verdict
that would heal the past abuses.
Her wounds were seldom visible,
the welts that ringed her throat now faded;
what proof had she to plead her case
that her essence was degraded?
Caustic words and days of silence
composed an ugly patchwork quilt
that wrapped her in his anger
that clung to her like silt.
The tongue, a mighty weapon, carves a crevice in the soul
it splits the personality so it never can be whole.

Land of the Empty

Live it up, laugh it up
You only live once
Get up off your ass
Don't be a dunce
Jump out of the woodwork
Put your dancing shoes on
Step up to the mic
'Fore your time is withdrawn.
The bland and the mundane
Might zap you tomorrow
In the land of the empty
There's no fun to be borrowed.
We each write our own page
In the book that steals time
In the land of the empty
Chapters end in flatline.

Dallas Hembra

Fire

Sienna peaks in distance loom
Devoid of life—now locked in gloom;
Through curtained fog, tired pupils focus
In search of sun and saffron crocus.

Drab olive usurps grass's mantle
Reducing it to umber's bramble;
Lush roses drained of crimson blood
Sucked dry—never again to bud.

Flame's raging tongue has licked its way
Across the forest's rich buffet;
It gorged and pillaged till it was spent
Echoes a toll, death's sad lament.

Book the Trip

The company I choose to keep on any given day
populates mind's pages as I hold the world at bay;
tucked between twin binders, these friends and foes alike
reveal their hidden secrets as they cause my heart to spike.
We roam the world to parts unknown;
with ease, we slip through time,
defying all that's relative
while costing not a dime.
I've fought alongside heroes, held their hands as they bled out
endured the wrath of evil through a portal labeled doubt;
on faded yellow parchment, I've spilled a lonely tear
in empathy for lovers, separated by their fears.

Dallas Hembra

A Field of Daisies

A daisy on a dreary day
blooms out of reach so far away.
What blue note plays a mournful song
that stretches thin this winter long?
Malaise, a dungeon dark creates
an atmosphere where hope abates
a grey sky smothers morning's light
I sink into soul's cold bruised night.
Where angels tread, I fall asleep
they pray to God my soul to keep
a field of daisies standing tall
emerge for one last curtain call.
The night retreats, the battle ends
translation's up to you, my friend.

Nightscapes

Your lips brush mine
Moment sublime
But cold the touch
Desired so much
The breath of all that used to be
Buried beneath our willow tree.
A chill runs up and down my spine
Uneasy thoughts I can't define
Suspended in this darkened room
My longing ebbs with the waning moon.
The truth I try to keep at bay
Will resurrect at break of day
You'll vanish into the unknown
And once again, I'll be all alone.

Stored Silence

Embedded in fright's memory
her door—his key
floorboards creaking
shadow seeking.
He slipped into her virgin bed
"Love you," he said.
She froze in place
he stroked her face.
He stretched his bow as he exhaled
she lay impaled—
accrued new fears
and stored the tears.

My Boring Poem

Buck naked on a nameless beach
I must vie for your attention,
But the shackles that enslave me
Remain a matter of contention;
The azure blue that drew the eye
Is muddied and opaque,
The sunset's rays extinguished
By the paling of daybreak;
The brush that paints my canvas
Soaking now in turpentine,
Is stripped of all its color
Emasculated by design;
The music has been muzzled
My embellishments abandoned;
Is it any wonder
That my fan base left me stranded?

Dallas Hembra

Accountability

If only, but, and just because—
The language of digression,
I borrowed and applied them all
To disguise my own transgressions.
Woven into my persona
Words that furnished alibis,
A few harmless variations
Of the facts—not really lies!
Intended as diversions
To escape the world's disdain
For a while, it seemed to work just fine
Relieving me of any blame.
When it's always someone else's fault
And I assume the victim's role,
Fine-tuning my integrity
No longer lives in my control.
But
Once the ifs and buts and just becauses
Can be dislodged and then replaced,
Accountability enables me
To reconstruct what they erased.

Success and Failure

When I reach into life's closet
To define myself each day,
Will I find the perfect label
My persona must convey?
Will the moniker that spells success
Be affixed to my façade,
Or will the rhythm of my swing and sway
Be out of sync, off-key, a tad bit odd?
Do my garments tell a story
Of a life that's full and rich,
A patchwork quilt of ups and downs
That are tucked into each stitch?
Will the blemishes and dreadful stains
That take up so much space
Define me as a failure, a loser, or a disgrace?
Or is success found in the weaving
Of the beauty and the beast,
The blending of both good and bad
Allowing their release?
The process is the journey
Up the hill, it bends—we swerve,
Till suddenly we see it—
Success embedded in the curves.

Communicate

Connecting in a meaningful way
Outside the chaos of the fray
Mending fencing with compromise
Muting the button on nonsense and lies.
Unfounded rumors designed to confound
Nullify efforts to seek common ground.
Imposing one's will through
Conversation will lead to solutions
Annihilation. So next time let's temper our
Talk with some wisdom
Expand our horizons and learn how to listen.

Truth

Turn delusion inside out
Run your conscience down the situation's fabric
Until the kinks and wrinkles relax. Allow the
Tailor to weave the thread through a tapestry of
Humility embossed in virtuous verity.

Dallas Hembra

Gratitude

Gather up the gossamer
Rhetoric and weave it into
Action
Temper the cheap talk;
Indict the insincerity.
Thank you yearns to walk the walk
Undressed—unadulterated—unfiltered
Doing good deeds, making sacrifices—
Empowering empty words.

Empathy

Emersion in the eye of the storm
Marries our shared experience. Dressed in
Priestly robes of grief and pain, we kneel at the
Altar of understanding as we
Travel together along the path of heartbreak
Huddled in harmony, bidding
Yesterday adieu.

Dallas Hembra

Cerebral Thinker

Calibrating
Each and every bit of information
Recalibrating—
Editing in the recesses of the
Brain where the thinker's true nature
Resides.
Academic meanderings un-
Leashed, unencumbered by the heart.
Tactical solutions
Hover on horizons where
Intuition has been
Nullified by the turn of a
Key, locking it out of the
Equation—
Reason ascending.

Apologies

Gather
apologies
from yesterday's ashes
then plant them in tilled arguments
to bloom.

Frozen

Fawn lies
in sweet repose
beneath the blizzard's breath—
remains, undetected until
spring's thaw.

Rebirth

Swallowed
the loneliness
born of a moonless night
as high-tide slaps morning awake
in rebirth.

Chameleon

Deep
inside
pain's casket,
a quivering
along love's fault line—
anxious to suppress it
before someone notices,
she plays the chameleon card
to camouflage the embarrassment
and slides his insult behind a fake smile.

Switching Tracks

Magicians levitate
The Buddhists meditate
Others celebrate
While I recalibrate.

The Precious Present

The day before tomorrow
holds the moments we misplaced
to reduce some of the sorrow
we've projected in its place
forever gone, the gift erased.

Dallas Hembra

Mindful Moment

Aging dad
attempts
to hang
houseplant
muscles atrophied
telltale tear
in a mindful moment.

Cocooned

An
embryo
blossoms
to its full potential,
cocooned
in a mother's
love

Dallas Hembra

Poets

He
Wraps his mind around words,
untangling kinetic disturbances
for the sake of structure.

She
Coaxes ideas to germinate—
reverberate,
stretch themselves into stanzas.

They
Paint forests framed in fantasies,
bleed
horrors etched in hauntings
laugh
humor crimped in comedy.
And

We
Whisper to your soul—
a language lettered in love.

Poetic Moments

We write poetic moments
When we offer a smile—
A gentle touch
Or a shoulder to cry on.

Mud-raking

In lieu of decorum,
Lame libelous leaders
Expose their defects
In mud-raking.

Serendipity

Serendipity
Stokes the embers
Left slumbering
In the recesses of rigidity.

Buoyancy

Light as a feather
Floating free in the breeze,
Humility drifts weightless
Untethered to ego.

Dallas Hembra

Twin Cycles

Remembrance etched in every wrinkle
rheumy blue pools reflect a soul
cleansed by the passing of time.
Unafraid he prepares
to meet his maker
but then decides
to take one
final
stroll.
Leaves
crunching
beneath his
feeble footsteps—
fall's crisp reminder
that lurking in the wings
winter waits impatiently
to wrap its cold white arms around
the last vestiges of autumn's warmth.

Obsessive/Compulsive

The bees are swarming inside my head
buzz-buzz-buzzing 'bout what you said
brain keeps working overtime.
Obsessive thoughts are not
a crime. OCD
my legacy
can't let go
one two
three—

Dallas Hembra

Kaleidoscopes

Gemstones spun in webs of gold
Savored by both young and old
Paint our world in varied hues
That chip away intrusive blues.
When blinded by adversity
We need color and diversity
Kaleidoscopes
kept close at hand
provide that need
if we get jammed.

If you enjoyed *Kaleidoscope*, you may enjoy reading *Shaking the Family Tree*.

There was a boogie man in the closet and its name was alcoholism.

This story is not for the faint of heart. *Shaking the Family Tree* is a personal memoir of a recovering alcoholic. It is interlaced with poetic offerings that take the reader to the heart and soul of the ramifications of the disease of alcoholism. Dallas's story is one of coming to terms with what has become her family's unfortunate legacy. She and her sister were raised by two loving parents who did the best they could. As young girls growing up, they never doubted for one moment whether or not they were loved, and were infused with a strong sense of family values.

Alcoholism wasn't a stranger to the family. It could be traced back for three generations and continues to reveal itself in three younger generations of Dallas's family. In her memoir, Dallas explains her battle with co-dependency and the genetic predisposition for alcoholism being the single thread that ties it all together of what made her life a living hell.

Dallas didn't give up. Although she wanted to kick the habit, it wasn't easy. With the help of a loyal sponsor, a lot of determination, and several hard lessons, Dallas now shares how she conquered her biggest demons and became a survivor of alcoholism.

About the Author

Kaleidoscope is Dallas's second book. Her first book was a personal memoir/poetry offering entitled *Shaking the Family Tree*. Published under Dallas H., it revealed her personal struggle with alcoholism, the genetic predisposition, and the ensuing family dynamics.

Dallas lives in the Northern Panhandle of West Virginia. When she isn't writing, painting, or supplementing her income by working part-time at a local bank, Dallas is updating her recovery blog. The mother of three sons, five grandsons, and two great-grandchildren, she views life through her own kaleidoscope, one honed from an attitude of gratitude.

Her poetry has been published in two anthologies, *Psycho Poetica*, and she is a regular contributor to the online weekly literary journal *Page & Spine*.

Dallas invites you to find her on Facebook @ AuthorDallasH, Twitter @DallasH01, or at her recovery blog at authordallash.com.

www.ingramcontent.com/pod-product-compliance
Lightning Source LLC
Chambersburg PA
CBHW052113110526
44592CB00013B/1590